THE Great Teas OF CHINA

西湖龍井

祁門紅茶

白茶

碧螺春

茉莉花茶

THE Great Teas OF CHINA

ROY FONG

Tea Journey Books
Oakland, California

Published by
Tea Journey Books
8451 Baldwin Street
Oakland, CA 94621

Cover and book design © Ayelet Maida
Produced by A/M Studios
Cover photograph of green tea garden © Roy Fong; tea leaves © George Post; teacup © Gaetano Kazuo Maida; author photograph © Jeni Fong
Text photographs of tea leaves and brewed teas © George Post, all other photographs © Roy Fong
Calligraphy © Yang Jing Rui
Maps © Rick Wheeler

ISBN 978-0-578-04195-7

Printed in the USA

Tea Journey Books saved the following resources by using New Leaf Reincarnation Matte, made with 100% recycled fiber and 50% post-consumer waste, processed chlorine free, and manufactured with electricity that is offset with Green-e® certified renewable energy certificates: 8 fully grown tress, 1,823 gallons of water, 4 million Btu, 399 pounds of solid waste, 674 pounds of greenhouse gases. (Calculations based on research by Environmental Defense and other members of the Paper Task Force.)

14 13 12 11 10 UNITED 1 2 3 4 5

Dedicated to my wife Grace,
my best friend and partner,
loving mom to our two daughters,
Courtney and Emily…
amazing Grace.

NOTES:

With regard to tea names, I have generally elected to represent the names of the teas discussed in the simplified Chinese characters and *pin yin* romanization of the People's Republic of China, where most of these teas originate. However, in the case of *puerh,* I made an exception to follow the spelling convention of the venerable Yunnan Tea Import & Export Corporation, which to this day controls a large share of the market for *puerh* tea. In any case, it's important for Western readers to remember that romanization of Chinese characters is only a concern for those who don't speak Chinese. Everyone involved with tea in China understands tea names and other terminology in the appropriate Chinese characters, and anyone who aspires to communicate in this marketplace must aim to connect their messages to the Chinese language in a direct, consistent, and transparent way.

With regard to place names, single word representation is used where it is more commonly accepted.

In the interest of providing useful reference for readers, every effort has been made to render the photographs of tea leaves and the infused tea as accurately as possible in terms of actual color and size (of the leaves).

Contents

Tea Regions

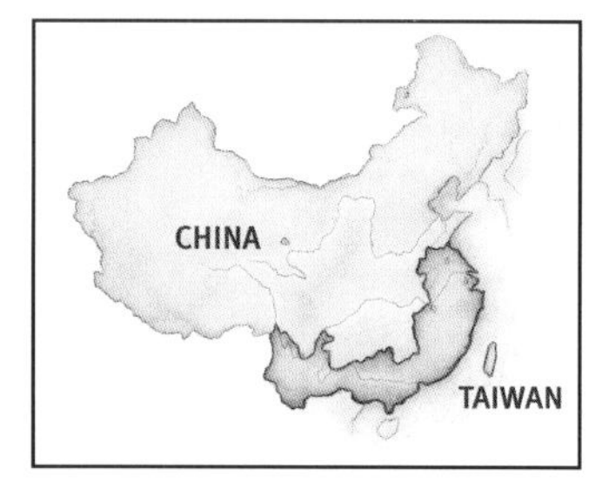

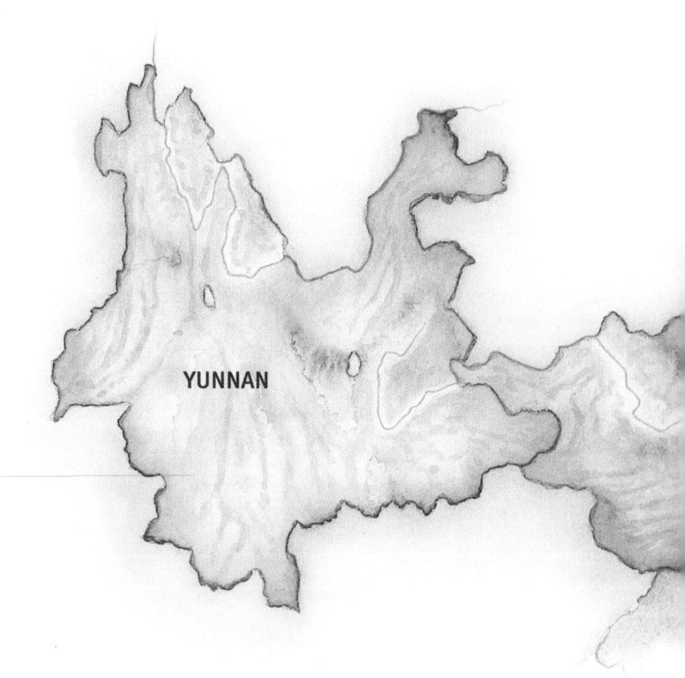

Primary Tea Producing Regions
of China and Taiwan

武夷岩茶

普洱茶

滇紅

鐵觀音

臺灣烏龍茶

Preface

The Chinese have a saying that reading ten thousand books can't compare to traveling ten thousand miles. Since my parents seem to have given the reading genes to my siblings, I have actually ended up traveling many tens of thousands of miles in the quest of the love of my life—tea. Learning as I grow, every trip brings new thoughts and ideas, new and unique experiences, new tea friends made, relationships renewed and solidified.

Ever since opening the first Imperial Tea Court in San Francisco in 1993, I have had the pleasure of countless moments of tea and conversation with many people, from devoted tea lovers to casual tea drinkers, from expert tea merchants to people just starting on the road towards a life with tea. One question often repeated over the years was, "why aren't you writing a book?"

Once I made the decision to go ahead with this book, I considered several different topics. Instead of writing about tea by categories or recounting the historic tales of tea, I decided to speak from my heart: I would write about great teas of China. The teas covered in this book are all well known but they might not necessarily be the most famous or the greatest in anyone else's eyes, just mine. These are teas that I've come to love and respect due to personal experience over a lifetime. Some of these teas I grew up with, others I only discovered as an adult, after I became devoted to learning the full diversity of *Camellia sinensis*. I have had the good fortune to travel the ten thousand miles of tea, and it is my privilege to be able to share these experiences with you.

I'd like to thank all of you who congregated to Imperial Tea Court, befriended us, and supported a tea merchant and his tiny tea company simply because he thought "yes, we can!"

Thanks are also in order for my friend Virginia Hines, who helped edit this book and supported Imperial Tea Court in so many different ways; also a note of thanks to Tano and Ayelet Maida for helping me believe that this book could be done and guiding me through this difficult process.

I would also like to thank Donald Wallis, who called me friend and founded the American and International Tea Masters Association during the early years of Imperial Tea Court.

And finally, I'd like to thank Mr. Chang Jin Qiang for his support and friendship while he was with the Yunnan Tea Import & Export Corporation, and for helping me make vital connections to tea during the early days of my tea career.

Roy Fong
November 2009

Introduction

China's tea culture as we know it today comes from the combined wisdom of countless thousands of people over the span of many centuries. Tea is one subject that you can safely declare cannot be learned in a mere lifetime. Tea lovers devote entire lives just to learning certain aspects of tea: the agriculture, the art of transforming the leaf from its natural state on the tea plant to the miracle we experience in the cup, the beauty and function of teaware, tea presentation, and preparation, not to mention the history of tea and the many great works of art and literature that depend on it. It can take a lifetime commitment just to scratch the surface of any of these facets of the tea experience. How can anyone ever imagine being able to learn it all?

I didn't recognize the significance at the time, but my destiny with tea began in childhood, in Hong Kong. I had a boring forty-five minute walk to school and often detoured past a group of day laborers waiting to be hired. They passed the time by making *gong fu cha* on a makeshift table, and when curiosity got the better of me I'd squat alongside them to watch the ritual that offered one of the day's scarce pleasures. Occasionally they would offer me a cup of what, to a six-year-old, smelled and tasted like the most wonderful tea on earth.

I'll never forget those memories, and I am sure this experience is the seed that blossomed into my passion for tea. After emigrating to the US and spending my teenage years in San Francisco, I dropped out of college and started working as an auto mechanic and tow truck driver. After a few years, I planned a month-long vacation back to Hong Kong. One day I happened to wander through the Sheung Wan district, where old teashops were still in abundance. There was an irresistible aroma, the smell of fresh tea being roasted over charcoal. I was drawn into a teashop and, without realizing it was a life-changing decision, decided to learn more about tea!

I spent the rest of the month going to every single teashop I could find. There was no tea too expensive or too unique to try at least once. In those days tea was purchased with virtually no instructions; buyers were expected to know what they wanted. In Hong Kong tea is almost a fact of life. Everyone drinks it, often with little conscious thought or care given to the details.

For me, that month in Hong Kong was spent in nine heavens. I visited and chatted with teashop owners, made friends, and learned trade secrets such as re-firing tea prior to sale, a practice that would later inspire me to fire my own Monkey-Picked Tie Guan Yin. I bought so much tea that I discarded all my belongings in order to fit more tea into my luggage. Back in San Francisco, I returned to my towing business and continued to buy tea from my new tea friends in Hong Kong. These relationships proved very important when I finally started to sell tea for a living. At that time, I

regarded myself as a serious tea drinker but nothing more. I never imagined that tea would one day be my vocation.

It was not until a month-long visit from Mr. Luo Qi Liang of Yunnan that the door to tea as a career was opened. I entertained this elderly gentleman by taking him to local restaurants and teashops without knowing that Mr. Luo was one of the most knowledgeable and influential tea persons I'd ever meet. We discussed tea constantly. I showed off my precious stocks of tea, and exchanged tea stories over many sessions of tea-drinking. Finally, prior to returning to China, Mr. Luo asked a simple, life-changing question: "You love tea so much, why aren't you in the tea business?"

Mr. Luo soon sent a full container load of *puerh* tea. My wife Grace and I started selling to Chinese restaurant distributors, and my new career as a tea merchant was underway. Some of the inventory from this original shipment formed the nucleus of my precious *puerh* collection.

When the concept of our first Imperial Tea Court was being developed in 1991, I called on my tea friends in Hong Kong to support me with their best products. This they did with very favorable terms and I am still grateful for their support. After we opened, however, I found that the standard practice of going to a tea broker to purchase available stock didn't allow any input from me, and I decided that in order to procure the best tea possible, I would have to understand each phase of tea production better. As my tea knowledge grew, I developed a practice that I continue even now: I target a tea that I am interested in and travel to the region where it grows. Instead of going right up to the farms, I spend time learning about local customs, food, and climate. Knowing what the people of the region eat and drink, understanding soil and weather conditions, and participating in the harvest and production all yield a deeper understanding of what gives a tea its unique character, and how to produce and prepare it in a way that best fulfills its potential.

My passion for tea continues to grow and I maintain my practice of doing something new each time I visit. I can't help but smile at the thought that this life in tea was set in motion by a six-year-old boy squatting beside the road in Hong Kong, hoping for a sip of tea…

Bai Hao Yin Zhen

ALSO KNOWN AS
Silver Needle

For well over a thousand years, China's southeastern coastal province of Fujian has been producing white tea. This type of tea is among the least processed of all the teas in this book, prized for its delicacy and subtle, yet complex, flavors. White tea is distinguished by two elements: the particular varietal—the *da ye* ("big leaf") variety, grown in Fujian's Zheng He and Fu Ding regions—and the production methods used.

REGION

Since the early Jia Qing era of the Qing dynasty (early nineteenth century), wild *da ye* teas called *cai cha* ("wild tea") were harvested early and made into white *ya cha* ("bud tea"). This *cai cha* variety was later cultivated and more widely grown in the Fu Ding area, in the northeastern part of Fujian. The cultivated version produced better white tips than *cai cha,* which

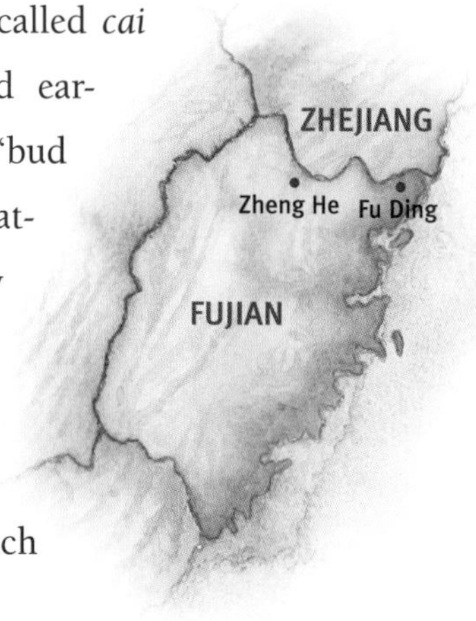

白茶

I used to think of white tea as the cheap shou mei *served in dim sum restaurants. Years ago, someone told me that the best grade of white tea was called* bai hao yin zhen, *or Silver Needle. When I finally had my first sip of Silver Needle, I remember saying to myself, "so what's the big deal?" As someone who adores big flavors such as* puerh *and* tie guan yin, *I simply did not give much thought to white tea. Not until I finally traveled to Fu Ding, the major white tea producing area in China, did I understand. When something is popular and has been famous for a long time, there is usually a good reason. Ancient Chinese believed that spring sunlight brings special life-giving properties. Is it any wonder that once I tasted a traditional spring-harvested and spring-sun-dried white tea, my horizon was changed and I began to understand?*

yields smaller, thinner tips. By the late nineteenth century cultivated tea had replaced *cai cha* as the variety of choice for white tea in Fujian. Around that time, the Zheng He region in northern Fujian began to cultivate and produce white tea, and since 1889 has been producing quality white tea by their own process. During the mid-nineteenth century Zheng He also produced some of China's best black teas using *da ye* leaves. This tea was called *min hong* ("Fujian red tea").

ON THE FARM

Generally, leaves covered completely in white down are considered the highest quality. There are usually two standards: *ya cha*, the unopened budding leaf, and *ye cha*, the fully opened leaf. *Ya cha* is commonly known as *bai hao yin zhen* ("White Hair Silver Needle") and is produced by one of two methods. In the partial sun-drying method of Fu Ding, buds are harvested in the spring. Thin layers of leaves are placed in bamboo baskets. The baskets are stacked in a wooden rack where the leaves air-dry naturally until they lose 80–90 percent of their moisture. The remaining moisture is then removed by warming the leaves in tall baskets over a charcoal fire. Modern tea factories use convection ovens to finish this final drying process to save time and to eliminate the chance of over-drying, which can lead to a smoky, burned flavor or darkening of the leaf. However, under-drying may result in underdevelopment of aromatics and discoloration.

In the complete sun-drying method of Zheng He, unopened leaves are placed in bamboo baskets, stacked, and moved to an area with indirect sunlight until they lose 70–80 percent of

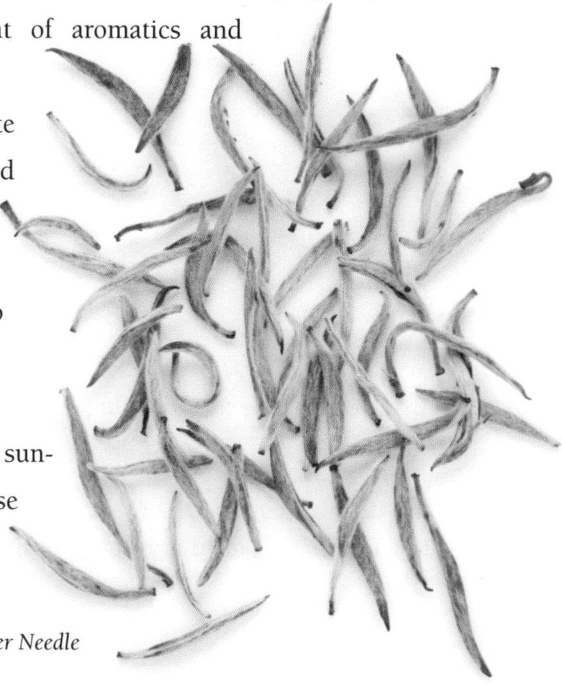

Imperial Silver Needle

their moisture. Then they are moved to direct sunlight until they're completely dry. It takes 7–8 kilograms of leaves to produce a kilogram of finished Zheng He *ya cha*. The full sun-drying process produces a less attractive but much better tasting tea; however, it is time-consuming and rarely practiced. During extreme humidity or rain, Zheng He tea may be fired dry, a technique that produces better looking tea but less flavor and aromatics.

Imperial Silver Needle

Bai Mu Dan

ALSO KNOWN AS
White Peony

Bai mu dan is another style of white tea. It is even more expensive and difficult to make than *bai hao yin zhen*.

REGION

Bai mu dan is produced in the same regions of Fujian Province as *bai hao yin zhen*.

ON THE FARM

In order to be classified as a true *bai mu dan*, the standard of "three whites" is required: the leaf set must possess one leaf bud covered in white down plus two leaves whose undersides are covered with white down and tops are dark green. The set is so delicately beautiful that it is referred to as "white peony," the

Imperial White Peony

Imperial White Peony

flower of wealth Chinese call the king of all flowers.

To meet this nearly impossible standard, the tea must be processed meticulously, beginning with selecting the right leaf sets during picking and carefully handling them to avoid bruising or damage that can result in unwanted color changes or incomplete sets. The leaf sets are withered indoors until their moisture content is around 30 percent; then they are fired at approximately 100°C to reduce moisture to about 10 percent. The leaves are allowed to cool completely, then there's a final firing at 80°C to dry them completely. The process not only heightens aromatics and flavor, but also preserves the green leaf color unique to *bai mu dan*. This rigorous traditional approach is rarely practiced today.

Sometimes you see *ye cha* with large, unattached, sometimes broken leaves. They should be classified as *shou mei* ("longevity eyebrows") or *gong mei* ("tribute eyebrows"), but are sometimes incorrectly called *bai mu dan*. These teas are processed with considerably less care and are generally finished by firing. As a result, *shou mei* and *gong mei* are darker in color and exhibit stronger but less complex flavors. Lower standard leaves are harvested later in the season, and since they are generally tougher, older leaves, after withering they are slightly rolled to further break down their cellulose structure and allow light oxidation. The leaves are then roasted dry. This is the standard generally classified simply as China white tea, which is often encountered in lower-priced, restaurant-grade teas.

Long Jing

ALSO KNOWN AS
Dragon Well

Long jing is one of the "Ten Most Famous" teas of China, noted for its "four uniques": light jade color in the cup, vegetal aroma, mellow chestnut-like flavor, and singular appearance with flat, straight, narrow leaves pointed at the tip, meticulously sorted to uniform size. This green tea is named after a spring with especially good water where a dragon-like rock was once discovered. The Qing dynasty Emperor Qian Long visited the area and fell in love with *long jing* tea, and he designated the tea bushes that gave him so much joy "Imperial" *long jing*.

REGION

Long jing is from the historically important tea producing areas surrounding Hangzhou (once the capital of Song dynasty China), in Zhejiang Province. The best *long jing* is produced in the scenic Xi Hu (West Lake) district, consisting of Shi Feng ("lion peak"), Mei Jia

西湖龍井

When I decided to open the first traditional Chinese teahouse in America, I naturally thought that long jing, *one of the world's most famous green teas, must be well represented. I ordered five kilos of the best* xi hu long jing *from a Hong Kong dealer. It took a full year to sell out that tea—it was extremely expensive but uninteresting, lacking all the key characteristics of a great* long jing*—so I went in search of the best* long jing *I could find.*

I met my friend Mr. Ye Yang, of the famed China Tea Research Institute in Hangzhou, the home of the great long jing. *The Tea Research Institute is located in one of the most prized* xi hu long jing *areas, Mei Jia Wu. Mr. Ye was in charge of the Institute's experimental tea farm and production facility.*

He took me through the entire xi hu *production area, explaining differences in varietals, different processing techniques, and the flavor and aromatic variations that result. With his help I was able to procure some of the best* long jing *tea ever made. I have returned to Hangzhou every year since that spring, always hopeful of finding even better tea. Mr. Ye has moved up and is no longer in charge of production, but we won't be running out of tea conversations anytime soon.*

Wu ("Mei family valley"), Long Jing ("Dragon Well"), and the Lin Yin Temple area.

ON THE FARM

Small shoots of *long jing* are picked by hand early in the spring. Those picked before the Qing Ming Festival (around April 5) are called *ming qian* ("before Qing Ming") and those picked for the following three weeks are called *gu yu* ("before the rain," *i.e.*, before the period of spring rain that begins the rice planting season). There are multiple grades of *long jing*, categorized by the time they're picked, type of leaf, shape, and uniformity of sorting.

The highest grade, *lian rui* ("lotus heart"), is very rare because of the extraordinary difficulty and expense of producing it. To make *lian rui* the first tiny, single buds are plucked from the tea bushes. Picking this early growth inhibits development of more leaves, reducing the plant's overall yield and increasing the value of *lian rui*. The next grade is *qi qiang* ("flag spear"), which comprises an unopened bud and a single leaf. The third grade is *que she* ("bird tongue"), a bud and

Lotus Heart Dragon Well

two leaves that are slightly curled like a small bird's tongue. The highest grades of *long jing* can require over 40,000 leaves to make a single pound of tea. As a result, they're very rare and expensive. Most of the *long jing* on the market is standard-grade, often machine-processed.

The best *long jing* is harvested during the spring, but a second harvest is sometimes produced on well-managed farms during the fall. While it tends to be more astringent, this crop can command a good price because it is fresh compared to tea made in the spring.

To produce *long jing*, after picking, the leaves are withered for 9–10 hours until they soften and moisture content is naturally reduced to approximately 70 percent. The evaporation of moisture also helps reduce the "green," or vegetal, flavors. Before oxidation begins the tea is pan-fired in a purpose-built wok. The heat prevents oxidation that would darken the leaf and change its flavor. It also removes moisture and makes the leaves pliable, which allows the teamaker to start to shape them and burn off their natural down by pressing them against the sides of the hot wok. When the leaves are dry enough and take on the correct shape, the tea is removed from the wok and allowed to cool. Later, another firing is performed to remove remaining moisture that would otherwise cause the tea to go stale or change color quickly. The final

Lotus Heart Dragon Well

firing also heightens aromatics and seals in flavor. After this second firing the tea is wrapped in rough paper and placed in an urn surrounded by packets of lime. The lime slowly draws out any remaining moisture so that only the true essence of the tea remains.

Bi Luo Chun

ALSO KNOWN AS
Green Conch Spring

Ancient Chinese called *bi luo chun xia sha ren xiang* ("astonishingly fragrant tea") because of its exquisite aroma. The name was later changed to *bi luo chun* ("green conch spring") when the tea was selected as tribute to the emperor; "astonishingly fragrant" was not a name deemed poetic enough for the court. The Chinese have many words to describe the color green. *Bi* in this case means a dark jade green, *luo* ("conch") describes the twisted spiral shape of the leaf, and *chun* ("spring") suggests a tea that's full of youthful energy. The character luo 螺 is sometimes changed to 罗, in which case it refers to the beautiful lacy dress of an ancient Chinese beauty, with the aim of adding even more elegance to this ultra elegant tea.

Bi luo chun has been prized since the Ming dynasty and was selected as a tribute tea during the Qing Kang Xi era (1661–1722). His grandson, Emperor Qian Long (1735–1795), was a great tea lover who reportedly enjoyed *bi luo chun* very much during his visit to the area.

REGION

Authentic *bi luo chun* comes from the Dong Ting Shan area in China's eastern province of Jiangsu. Dong Ting Shan is situated around Tai Hu (Lake Tai), China's largest freshwater lake. The mist and fog created by the large body of water help regulate temperature and humidity. These conditions, along with the naturally acidic soil there, help produce the qualities of this exceptional tea. Unfortunately, *bi luo chun*'s high value encourages counterfeits from many areas.

ON THE FARM

Bi luo chun is typically harvested early in spring, and like *long jing*, is most prized if picked just prior to Qing Ming. *Ming qian bi luo chun* is the most expensive. Anything harvested after Qing Ming is considered *gu yu* tea. The *gu yu* harvest continues until around April 20. Tea harvested during

Imperial Bi Luo Chun

碧螺春

It was not until after a few years in the tea business that I met this great tea close-up. A trip to a bi luo chun *tea farm was arranged by my friend Chen Nong, whose former sister-in-law was a city official from Shanghai. She arranged for me to meet with city officials from Yixing and also to meet with some famous Yixing teapot artists. Since Yixing is very close to Tai Hu, where the best* bi luo chun *is grown, I naturally asked to visit one of the most noted tea farms there.*

I arrived at the farm in mid-afternoon and was greeted by the owner and offered a glass of tea from that morning's production. Hot water was poured into a tall glass and a handful of tiny dark green and twisted leaf sets added to the water. The leaves slowly infused and gently spiraled and sank to the bottom of the glass, opening up into small flower-like sets as they descended. The aroma of fresh, sweet green tea filled the air. I waited until almost all the leaves settled in the bottom of the glass and took a sip. I still remember that silky soft, juicy mouth-feel without any hint of bitterness, the sweetness that slowly but surely filled my mouth and seemed to fill my whole being. All I could say to myself at that time was a big inward "WOW!"

this period may also be called *yu qian* ("before the rain") tea. *Yu qian* tea is still considered high quality. Anything harvested after April 20 is called *yu cha* ("rain tea") and is considered poor quality. Leaf sets consisting of a single down-covered bud and a newly opened leaf are picked.

Picking occurs early in the morning (5:00–9:00), then the leaves are allowed to wither indoors for 6–7 hours to soften them. The *sha qing* process (applying heat to arrest oxidation) is done in a large wok at high temperature (190°–200°C) for about 3–5 minutes. The high-temperature firing cooks the leaves through and further softens them. The temperature is then lowered to 70°–75°C, the tea is rolled rigorously by hand, and moisture is reduced to approximately 30 percent. The leaves are allowed to cool and one last pan firing is done to further dry and shape the tea; the final firing also ensures that the tiny down remains attached to the leaves and that the leaves do not change color. Finally, the tea is roasted until it's completely dry, a process that heightens the aromatics and leaf color and seals in flavor. It takes over 70,000 hand-picked leaf sets to make about one pound of high quality *bi luo chun*.

Imperial Bi Luo Chun

元和道士姚合　乞新茶
嫩绿微黄碧澗春
採時聞道斷葷辛
不將錢買將诗乞
借問山翁有幾人
楊錦銳书

Qi Xin Cha (Begging for Fresh Tea)
by Yao He

Tender green and pale yellow in the jade-like spring leaf
Harvesting tea brings enlightenment, cleansing mind and body
Instead of money, I beg for tea with poems
May I ask, how many people are like me?

Calligraphy by Yang Jing Rui
Yao He was a Daoist hermit who lived during the Tang dynasty.

Mo Li Hua Cha

ALSO KNOWN AS
Jasmine Tea

Since the Tang dynasty, people have been enhancing the taste of tea by adding herbs and spices. Records indicate that during the Song dynasty, tea production involving flowers to improve flavor and aromatics had become popular, but not until the Ming dynasty did jasmine tea production become more systematic. From carefully choosing the right kind of tea to be scented to choosing the right flowers at the right time, formulas were developed and continued to advance. During the Qing dynasty's Xian Feng era in the mid-nineteenth century, large-scale, systematic production of jasmine tea began in Fuzhou, the capital of Fujian.

REGION

Although produced in many tea-growing regions, the best jasmine teas are traditionally produced in Fuzhou. Due to the current booming economy and rising cost of labor, however, the

茉莉花茶

Like a lot of tea enthusiasts, I initially gave jasmine tea no respect. Being exposed only to poor quality jasmine teas early in life did not help my view. Certainly one of the most popular teas worldwide, jasmine continues to be considered unworthy of serious attention.

In truth, no one can make great jasmine simply for money. The amount of hard work and devotion required to make great jasmine tea is almost unparalleled.

Fuzhou area is now only producing the highest quality jasmines; the bulk now come from the Hengxian County of Guangxi Province. Jasmine blooms earlier there and labor costs are lower. The trend is expected to continue until eventually Guangxi takes over virtually all jasmine production.

ON THE FARM

Producing fine jasmine tea starts by selecting the best green tea in early spring. Tender leaf buds from Fujian's Fu Ding area are considered the best base material for great jasmines. This green tea features nice white tips with good amounts of down that absorb aromatics well; also, the tippy green tea from Fu Ding is less astringent and well suited for scenting. The spring-harvested leaves are withered indoors, pan-fired to stop oxidation, then rolled into shape and roasted dry. This type of green tea is called *hong qing* ("roasted green").

The finished tea is cleaned and sorted into different grades and carefully stored until the jasmine blooms in early summer. When the jasmine harvest begins, unopened flower buds are picked early in the morning and delivered to tea factories in late afternoon (modern factories sometimes buy jasmine blossoms in open wholesale markets). The flowers are laid on the ground to allow them to open naturally. Their high moisture content causes fermentation and heat, which forces the buds open. The piles of flowers are watched carefully to avoid over-fermenting. The flowers are turned and flipped in the air to release moisture and prevent too much heat from accumulating, which would cause the loss of aromatics, and "burning" (the flower turning brown). This process generally lasts until very late at night. Finally, when most of the flowers are open, they are machine-sifted to remove unopened buds.

Imperial Jasmine Pearls

At the same time, the spring-harvested tea is taken from storage and re-roasted to remove staleness and ensure that it's completely dry and ready to absorb the jasmine fragrance.

The flowers are then mixed with freshly fired green tea in small batches. Each batch is watched carefully and turned from time to time to release heat. This process continues through the night, allowing the tea to slowly absorb the nectar and essence of the flowers. The tea and the flowers are separated in the morning. The tea is roasted dry once again to remove the excess moisture received from the flowers and further eliminate some of the leaves' own astringency. This scenting procedure may be repeated as many as seven times, each time completing a cycle of fluid exchange from the flower to the leaf, ensuring the complete saturation of floral aromatics.

When the final scenting is completed, a final step called *ti hua* ("floral pickup") is done. *Ti hua* includes a light roasting to reduce moisture to under 5 percent, and the tea is again mixed with freshly opened flowers for a few hours.

Imperial Jasmine Pearls

Ti hua saturates the leaf with floral aromatics externally, to heighten the initial aromatic appeal. The entire process must be done so that the color of the leaf remains green without losing the white color of the fuzzy tips. Jasmine teas are often hand-fashioned into various shapes to add visual interest. One of the most popular is called Jasmine Pearl, or sometimes Jasmine Dragon Phoenix Pearl. These small, tightly rolled balls are created in the spring, when the tea is fresh. They're produced by selecting only spring-harvested single tips (no open leaves). The tips are softened by pan firing, then a few are hand-rolled into a "pearl" shape, held together by the leaves' juices. They are stored carefully until summer for scenting. Sometimes teamakers will use long rolls of cotton paper to hand-wrap each individual pearl. The pearls are unwrapped and scented when the jasmine blossoms become available.

Tie Guan Yin

ALSO KNOWN AS

Iron Goddess of Mercy

Tie guan yin, a renowned oolong from Fujian's Anxi County, bears a name and legend that relate to the Buddhist embodiment of compassion, Guan Yin. According to one of the many stories about the origin of this tea, one night, Guan Yin appeared to a farmer in a dream and told him that behind the local Buddhist temple was a treasure to be enjoyed for generations if he shared it generously. What he found was a tea plant, and his devotion was rewarded with this uniquely flavored varietal. The word *tie* ("iron") may refer either to the reddish, oxidized edge of the processed leaf or the dark color of a well-fired leaf. *Tie guan yin* is known for its thick leaves, full of flavor that mix floral notes with nuttiness and occasionally an exotic peachiness, as well as a lingering, sweet aftertaste.

REGION

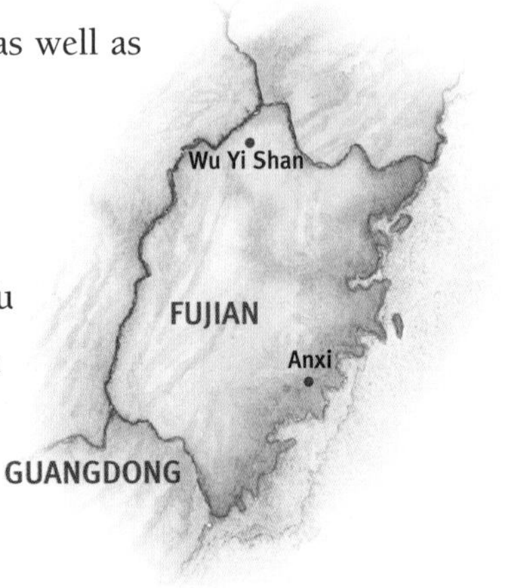

Tie guan yin originated in the Wu Yi Shan area of northwestern Fujian and a small quantity is still harvested and produced there. The best *tie guan yin* is now grown in and around Anxi County, with a small quantity produced to the south, in Guangdong Province.

ON THE FARM

The best *tie guan yin* is harvested in the spring and late fall. Leaf sets consisting of three leaves and a bud are picked and allowed to wither outdoors. They are raked and turned from time to time to equalize withering; when they start to soften they are moved indoors and placed in flat bamboo baskets. Soon the leaves start to release a fruity, floral fragrance as they continue to wither, a sign of enzymatic action. Next, they are placed in a large bamboo drum and turned so that they tumble and bruise. The leaves are then pan-fired (traditionally in a large wok, but modern teamakers use a heated stainless steel drum) to arrest oxidation. This *sha qing* process also cooks the tea leaves through, removes some of the harsh, bitter grassiness, and makes the leaves pliable. Then the leaves are placed into a machine to be rolled and shaped. Traditionally, rolling and wok-firing was done by hand; the softened

Jade Tie Guan Yin

鐵觀音

I immigrated to the US when I was about thirteen and it wasn't until my early twenties that I returned to Hong Kong for a vacation. The neighborhood I grew up in had totally changed and was unrecognizable, so I decided to look for signs of the Hong Kong of my childhood. The search took me to Sheung Wan, the district where antique and teashops were still in abundance. I walked around that area aimlessly one day and my nose caught a distinctive aroma unlike anything I'd ever encountered. I followed the fragrance and walked into a tiny teashop. The owner was doing the final roasting of his tie guan yin, *and I knew right then that my life would never be the same again…*

and rolled leaves were rolled tightly in muslin and vigorously rolled by hand and foot.

The pan-firing and rolling can go many rounds, until the teamaker decides the tea is ready. Finally, the leaves are roasted dry, then sorted, with stems and broken leaves removed. A final firing is often done prior to sale.

Tie guan yin may be brewed many ways, but traditional *gong fu* preparation using a small *yixing* pot produces the best results.

Jade Tie Guan Yin

范仲淹 鬥茶歌

年年春自東南來

建溪先暖冰微開

溪邊奇茗冠天下

武夷仙人從古栽

楊錦銳書

Dou Cha Ge (Tea Competition Ballad)

by Fan Zhong Yan

Spring comes from the southeast every year

Jian Xi warms first and the ice begins to crack

The tea grown next to this spring is the best under heaven

The immortals from Wu Yi planted it from ancient times

Calligraphy by Yang Jing Rui

Fan Zhong Yan was a scholar during the Song dynasty.

Wu Yi Yan Cha

ALSO KNOWN AS
Wu Yi Cliff Tea

Oolong tea from Wu Yi Shan (Wu Yi Mountain) is noted for its big, weighty flavor, known as *yan yun*. *Yan* refers to the region's cliffs and large boulders that partially shade the tea and retard growth but yield stronger leaves; *yun* is a sensation similar to a musical note that evokes serenity. The full range of Wu Yi teas extend from a green, lightly oxidized leaf to a dark, high-fired, and highly oxidized leaf. Flavors range from strong, bold, full-bodied earthiness to sweet, clean, and floral notes, or anywhere in between. There are more than a hundred varieties of *yan cha*. The four most notable are *da hong pao* ("big red robe"), *bai ji guan* ("white cock's comb"), *shui jin gui* ("golden water turtle"), and *tie luo han* ("iron arhat").

People of the Wu Yi Shan area eat strong, spicy foods to combat the cool, damp winters and hot, humid summers, and they prefer their tea very strong as well. Most Wu Yi oolongs are geared towards that flavor profile. High oxidation and high roasting temperatures create a dark leaf with hearty flavor. The more subtle of the Wu Yi teas are not as popular and are less well known, but are by no means lower in quality or flavor.

REGION

Wu Yi Shan has been producing famous tea since the Tang dynasty. Its teas are reputed to be the first exported to the West, during the 1600s. The best Wu Yi oolongs are produced in the Wu Yi Shan region. Tea produced there is considered *zheng yan* ("authentic *yan cha*"); tea produced near the area is called *ban yan* ("half *yan cha*"), while tea produced in the neighboring lowlands is called *zhou cha* ("regional tea"). Since the Tang dynasty, Wu Yi Shan has been producing excellent tea; noted poets including Li Po and Fan Zhong Yan have written beautiful poems about Wu Yi tea.

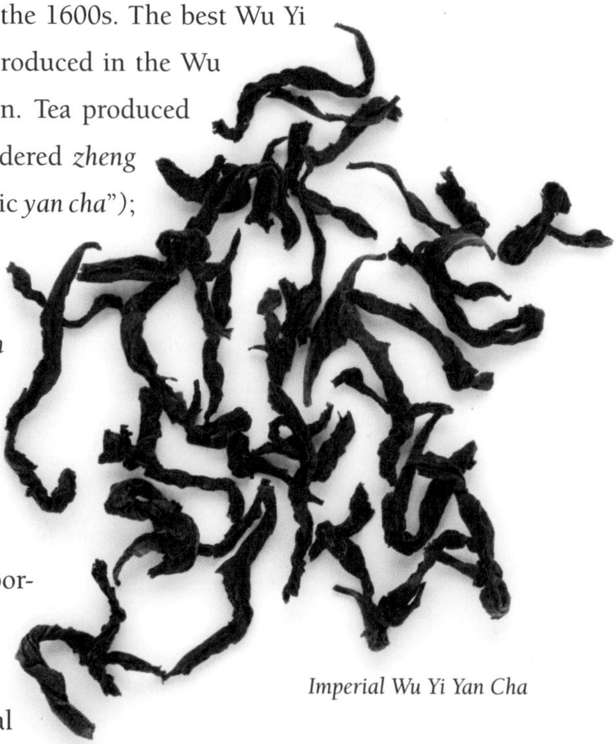

Imperial Wu Yi Yan Cha

武夷岩茶

I am not sure when the name Wu Yi Shan was imprinted on my memory, but it seems that I've always known that name and had a special feeling for it. When I met and received an invitation to visit with Mr. Chen Yin, an official who resides in Wu Yi Shan, I jumped at the chance. In the 1980s, a visit to Wu Yi Shan was no cakewalk. First there was a train ride of around eight hours from Fujian's capital, Fuzhou, and then a two-hour drive into the city of Wu Yi Shan. There were no hotels at the time, just a state-owned guest house. I knew I was in trouble when I took the mosquito net down and along with it came a cloud of dust. There was a large hole in the screen and mouse droppings on the pillowcase and yellow spots on the sheets. I was so exhausted from the long day of traveling that I simply turned the pillow over and slept with my clothes on. The next morning, I woke up with two badly swollen arms from mosquito bites; having covered my head with my arms to ward off the biting insects, my arms bore the brunt of their hunger.

Early in the morning, I made my pilgrimage to the site of the ancient tea bushes called da hong pao *("big red robe"), reputed to have saved the life of an aspiring scholar who fell ill on the way to his Imperial Examination. Local monks served the poor scholar with this tea and cured him. Later he returned as an official of the court and paid tribute to the tea bushes that saved his life by covering the bushes with his official red robe. The hike to the site was long and difficult under hot and humid conditions, but the breathtaking scenery of Wu Yi Shan never failed to keep me going. Virtually every turn presents a different view of natural beauty. I finally arrived and sat in front of those ancient bushes and drank tea grown in the gardens directly below, the tea brewed with exceptionally clean and delicious water from the spring there. At that moment, all the minor sufferings to get there were forgotten.*

Later that day I took the famous Wu Yi Shan bamboo raft trip, an hour of pure visual delight floating down the Nine Bends River with all the natural beauty around seemingly unchanged for hundreds, perhaps thousands, of years. What amazed me most was that in the late afternoon you can actually smell the floral fragrance from tea bushes grown on the hillsides along the river. The phenomenon of strong afternoon sun and cooler evening air releasing aromatics from tea bushes only seems to happen in Wu Yi Shan.

ON THE FARM

The production of Wu Yi *yan cha* has changed from steamed green tea a thousand years ago in the Tang dynasty, to what we would recognize as oolong tea by the end of the Ming dynasty. Ming-era production methods are still being used in Wu Yi Shan. The best teas are harvested either in the morning from 9:00–11:00 or in the afternoon from 2:00–5:00. Sets of three or four leaves are harvested and placed in flat bamboo baskets or on bamboo mats under indirect sunlight to allow moisture to evaporate; this withering process allows oxidation to begin and also reduces the bitter green flavor of the tea. Depending on the amount of tea, temperature, and sunlight, as well as the quality of tea, the initial withering process can take from 30 minutes to 2 hours. The tea is then moved indoors to continue withering.

Imperial Wu Yi Yan Cha

After it's fully withered, the tea is placed in large bamboo drums for 5–7 rounds of tumbling, which bruises the leaves to enhance oxidation. For each session the rolling time is increased and the waiting period before the next tumbling is also increased. In all, rolling can take as much as 12 hours to complete. Next, to soften the leaves, remove moisture, and stop further oxidation, the leaves are pan-fired in either large woks or temperature-controlled steel drums. The tea is rolled by machine and shaped, then roasted in a bamboo basket to

70 percent dry, allowed to cool, and sorted to remove broken leaves and stems. Finally, the tea is roasted completely dry.

Wu Yi *yan cha* is still produced with traditional methods that oxidize the tea to a much higher degree than tea such as *tie guan yin*. Wu Yi teas are also not rolled as tightly as *tie guan yin*, allowing the final firing to penetrate the leaves and turn them dark brown. The brewed leaf reveals reddish edges and the liquor from these higher oxidized teas can range from deep yellow to dark reddish brown, with the reddish color reflecting greater oxidation.

Lapsang Souchong

This black tea from the Wu Yi Shan area is well known in the West from the days of the Dutch and British empires, but is not popular in China. First there is the issue of name: the Chinese know this tea as *zheng shan xiao zhong* ("true mountain, small variety"). Then there is the issue of quality. Most of the smoky teas called lapsang souchong are from low-lying areas such as Fu An and Zheng He, where they are known as *xiao zhong*. Better examples designated *zheng shan xiao zhong* are from higher altitude areas such as Chong An, Jian Yang and Guang Ze, but until recently, were rarely exported. The distinctive smoky fragrance comes from the use of pine wood to produce high-temperature smoke to induce withering and drying in the cool mountain climate.

A fruity, *long yan*-like flavor can be detected if this tea is brewed for a short infusion with medium hot water.

Taiwan Oolongs

ALSO KNOWN AS

Bai Hao, Bao Zhong, Dong Ding

Taiwan has been producing great oolongs for well over a hundred years. There are three primary styles: *dong ding* ("frozen summit"), *bao zhong* ("wrapped style"), and Formosa Oolong. In the West, *bao zhong* is sometimes known by the antiquated term "pouchong." Formosa Oolong is also known as *bai hao* ("white fur") oolong or Oriental Beauty.

REGIONS

During the Jia Qing era of the Qing dynasty (early nineteenth century), oolong tea seeds were brought to Taiwan from Wu Yi Shan and planted with great success in the northern part of the island, a region now known as Ping Lin or Wen Shan. The offspring of these teas have now prospered into *bao zhong* and Formosa Oolong, which are still mostly grown around Wen Shan and Ping Lin, as well as *dong ding*-

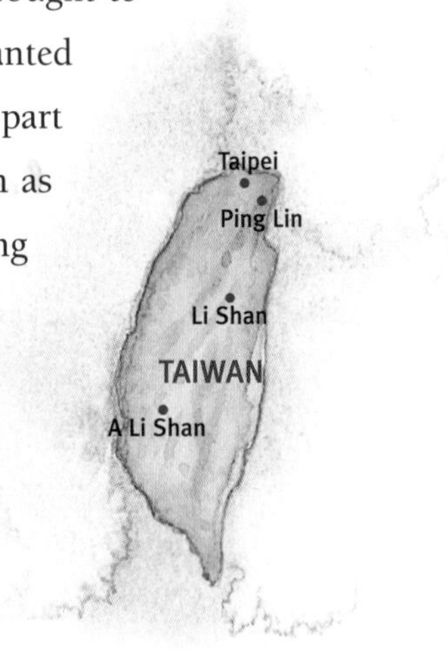

style oolongs most successfully grown in Lu Gu and Song Bai Keng (Song Bo Village) near southcentral Nantou County. There, oolongs grown at lower altitudes are mostly harvested by machine and rolled into tight "pearl" shapes by special rolling devices. Today there are many hybrid varietals of Taiwan oolongs.

Other regions famous for high-grown *dong ding*-style oolongs include A Li Shan, Li Shan, and Shan Lin Xi. In these and other choice areas, most of the oolongs are harvested and rolled into tight balls by hand. Teas from these regions command a much higher price and in general are considered very high quality.

ON THE FARM

Bao zhong is generally the least oxidized style of oolong from Taiwan. Like most other Taiwan oolongs, *bao zhong* is harvested almost all year long. The season from late March to early May is considered spring harvest; from late May to August is summer harvest (usually the least valuable); and mid-August to late October yields the autumn harvest. The winter harvest is picked from late October to mid-November and to

臺灣烏龍茶

I traveled to Taiwan the year after I rediscovered tie guan yin *in Hong Kong. Although I did not know many people in Taiwan at that time, tea was not difficult to find—virtually every corner of every city on the island offers a teashop of some kind, and there are numerous* cha yi guan, *teahouses with sit-down tea tastings, music, and other related traditional offerings. The people of Taiwan take tea drinking to new heights, with their specially designed teawares and a more formal adaptation of China's* gong fu *tea practice, all intertwined a bit with Japan's version of tea philosophy. There is a uniquely Taiwan experience when it comes to tea, not to mention some of the greatest oolongs on the planet.*

Not until I became a tea merchant did I finally meet a Taiwanese tea grower, Mr. Liao Ming Tsung, who owns the Hua Shan Tea Factory in Nantou County. I spent an entire night with him, talking, drinking tea, and going out to the factory to look at the teas at different stages of processing. The twenty-four hours of nonstop work offered me first-hand experience; cupping the tea during each step of its processing gave me an in-depth understanding of how flavors developed and changed. It was one of the most important tea lessons of my life.

some is the most desirable. Typically, the spring and winter harvests of *bao zhong* are most flavorful, with good floral notes. The high value placed on the winter harvest is due to its more prominent floral character, rich, chewy mouthfeel, and the lack of astringency.

Imperial Bao Zhong

Traditionally, oolong is harvested later in the day so that the first outdoor withering can be done near the evening, when the sun is low. However, modern production demands more efficiency and freshly picked leaves are now delivered to the factory throughout the day. Upon arrival they're laid on bamboo mats outdoors to start the first withering process, sometimes with a nylon sunscreen blocking direct sunlight during midday withering to keep the temperature down. During this withering process the leaves are gently turned 2–3 times with bamboo rakes to release 5–10 percent of their moisture. The tea is moved indoors for further withering. Thin layers of leaves are placed in flat bamboo baskets, which are stacked in a rack to allow air ventilation. From time to time the baskets are shaken and tossed gently to help release moisture evenly. High-quality modern tea factories do their indoor withering in air-conditioned rooms for better control of temperature and moisture. Generally the withering room is kept at around 20°C. The leaves start to soften, releasing a lychee-fruit-like aroma.

Imperial Green Oolong

The next step is tumbling, when the leaves are placed into a large bamboo drum that's turned so that the leaves tumble inside and are lightly bruised. After bruising the leaves are left to oxidize for a period of time. The tea then goes through a stage of *sha qing* pan-firing to arrest oxidation, soften the leaves, and lower moisture content by another 35–40 percent. Next the softened leaves are lightly rolled in a special machine, allowed to cool, then rolled with more pressure until they take on the desired shape. The rolling process also releases juice from the leaves and breaks down their cellulose structure, allowing for quicker release of aromatics and flavors during infusion. Finally, the tea is roasted at high temperature, allowed to cool, then finished at a lower temperature.

Bao zhong leaves appear long, twisted, and dark bluish green. Because of this color some tea merchants have started to call *bao zhong* and other high-grown Taiwan oolongs "blue oolong."

The processing for *dong ding* style oolongs is similar but the oxidation level is generally a bit higher. *Dong ding* oolongs are allowed to oxidize until the leaves become darker but the process is stopped before they turn reddish brown. The rolling process is much more rigorous: the leaves are wrapped tightly in a nylon bag, heated, and rolled as many as ten times; the finished result is leaves rolled into very tight balls.

Production of Formosa Oolong *(bai hao)* requires high oxidation to achieve the almost black tea-like color and honey-like floral notes. Formosa Oolong usually consists of tender leaf sets with unopened tips still attached. They undergo longer withering times both outdoors and indoors,

Imperial Bai Hao Oolong

with far more oxidation time allowed between each bamboo drum tumbling. Pan-firing occurs at a lower temperature to reduce moisture content by 40 percent or so. The leaves are then wrapped in a moistened cloth for about 20 minutes to soften them before the next rolling, a process that helps keep the fragile tips intact. The rolling process is performed gently to avoid breaking the leaf sets. The tea is then carefully roasted dry to produce a light reddish-brown leaf with white tips.

The most prized Formosa Oolong is produced from leaves that have been briefly colonized by a tiny insect called the tea green leafhopper, which lays its eggs on the young leaves. These insects can reproduce up to 14 times per year, with the heaviest infestation from May to July (harvest time for Formosa Oolongs). Infestation causes the leaf to wilt and turn brown, eventually killing it. But tea made with leaves harvested during the early period of infestation exhibits fragrances of honey and flowers that are unique to Formosa Oolong. The processed leaves have silvery-white tips and a dark reddish tone.

Imperial Bai Hao Oolong

Dian Hong

ALSO KNOWN AS
Yunnan Black

Yunnan's famous *puerh* tea has been in production and trade since the Tang dynasty more than a thousand years ago. Not until 1938, however, with the official establishment of the Yunnan Tea Import & Export Corporation, did the production of *dian hong,* or Yunnan black tea, begin (*dian* is an alternate name for Yunnan). The first batch of approximately 2,500 kilograms was produced in Yunnan's Feng Qing and Fo Hai (now called Meng Hai) areas. It was sold to England via a Hong Kong trading company with great success. It was reputed that the royals prized and treasured this great black tea from China. However, shortly afterward, war with Japan, China's civil war, and ongoing turmoil in China practically brought tea production in Yunnan to a standstill. Not until 1987

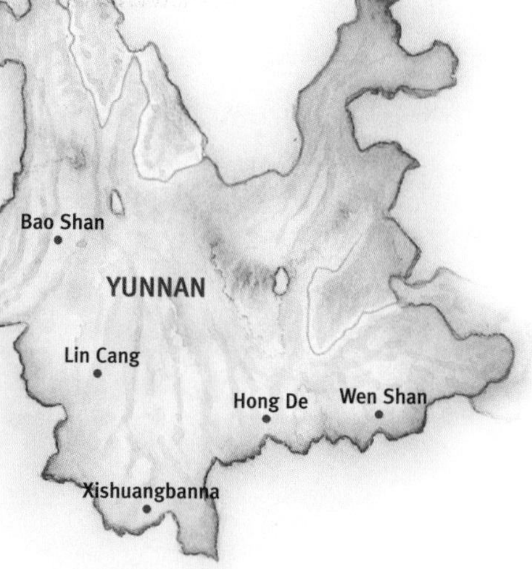

滇红

I'd heard many descriptions of Yunnan black tea—peppery, spicy, intense ruby-red color, etc., but no one had ever used the term elegant when talking about this tea. Imperial Yunnan Black, however, is nothing less than elegant. Beautifully hand crafted, it has all the elements that make Yunnan tea special, but more: the mouth-feel is simply exquisite, the finish long, clean, and sweet, unlike any other black tea in the world.

I traveled to Yunnan to attend the fiftieth anniversary of the Yunnan Tea Import & Export Corporation to see for myself how this wonderful tea was being produced. If you ever get to stand in the middle of a black tea factory with tons of tea being fermented, you're not likely to be the same ever again.

did Yunnan resume full tea production, with Yunnan black tea accounting for approximately 20 percent of the total.

Dian hong is known for its tightly rolled leaf and oily, blackish luster, with a profusion of golden tips. These golden tips vary in color, with the spring harvested ones being mild golden yellow. Summer-harvest tips tend to be larger and are known as "chrysanthemum" golden yellow tips, while the fall harvest brings the most spectacular, reddish-yellow golden tips. *Dian hong* yields a robust deep ruby-red liquor with a unique fragrance and taste notes unlike any other black tea in the world.

REGION

The name Yunnan means "Southern Clouds" and designates a high, mountainous area in China's Southwest that produces some of the world's most extraordinary teas, ranging from *chao qing cha* ("pan-fired green tea") to *shai qing cha* ("sun-dried green tea," the base for *puerh*), to *dian hong* (Yunnan black tea). Over three-quarters of Yunnan black tea grows in the west of the province, a nineteen-county area in the prefectures of Lin Cang, Bao Shan, and De Hong encompassing half of Yunnan's tea acreage and total tea output. The remaining *dian hong* comes from twenty-two southerly counties in the prefectures of Si Mao, Xishuangbanna, Hong De, and Wen Shan. China has designated Xishuangbanna the "birthplace of the world's tea trees" because wild tea trees over fifty feet tall and hundreds, even a thousand years old survive there.

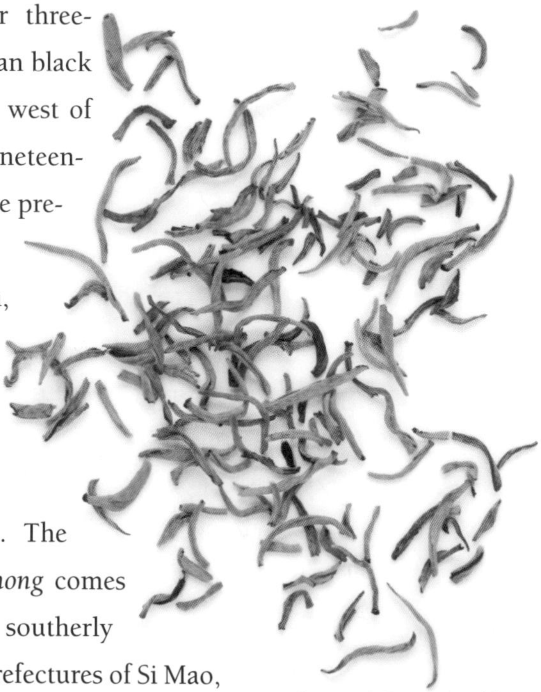

Imperial Yunnan Gold

ON THE FARM

Dian hong are separated into congou (leaf grade) and broken (fannings, CTC, BOP). There are six grades of congou; in

addition, the all gold-tip Yunnan black tea is called Imperial Dian Hong.

The production of leaf-grade tea starts with the selection of fresh leaves to be harvested, from a single unopened bud to a bud and three leaves, depending on the time of year and quality desired. After leaves are picked they are set to wither indoors or in indirect sunlight. There are two different withering methods: natural withering, where a thin layer of leaf is laid on bamboo mats, and trough withering, where freshly picked leaves are placed into a "fermenting" trough with pipes that bring in warm air to accelerate the process when needed. After withering the leaves are rolled several times to break down their cellulose structure, preparing them for further oxidation. This step is also very important for the development of good aromatics as well as the color and shape of the final product.

Imperial Yunnan Gold

After rolling, the leaves are fermented in the trough, a process that develops the unique color and flavor of *dian hong*. Correctly fermented *dian hong* develops a mature fruity fragrance. The harsh grassiness of fresh leaves has completely dissipated; the finished leaves have completely turned brownish red. Finally, the leaves are dried with care so that *dian hong*'s trademark golden down is preserved. The highest quality *dian hong* is a gold-tip only version; for this grade of tea, we feel that only skilled *gong fu* preparation will do it justice. However, the *gaiwan* method can also serve the purpose. The truth is that this grade of tea is so rare and exceptional that no matter how you decide to treat it, it is likely that it will deliver more than you expect.

black

Qi Men

ALSO KNOWN AS
Keemun

One of the most celebrated black teas from China comes from Qi Men County of Anhui Province. *Qi men* (sometimes known in the West by the antiquated name "keemun") is among the oldest black teas produced in China. Prior to the late Qing dynasty, Qi Men was producing good quality green tea. In 1876 production of black tea began, modeled after methods used in neighboring Fujian. The resulting tea was extremely popular and eventually became one of the world's most noted black teas, often the dominant component of "breakfast" blends.

REGION

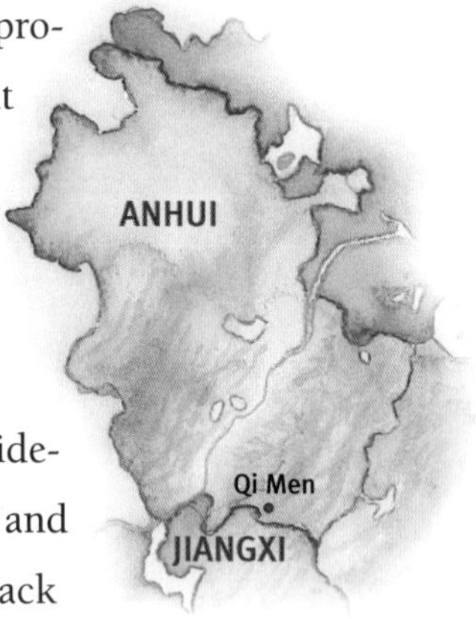

Anhui Province is a major tea producing area, the source of excellent green teas such as *huang shan mao feng, liu an gua pian,* and *tai ping hou gui,* in addition to *qi men.* Although the best quality *qi men* comes from Qi Men County, it's widely grown in neighboring counties and as far away as Jiangxi Province. Black teas of this style produced outside of Qi Men County are sometimes called Anhui black tea.

ON THE FARM

Qi men is produced from a *xiao ye* ("small leaf") varietal that typically yields a dark finished leaf. A good quality *qi men* has the quality Chinese call *bao guang* ("treasured luster"). *Qi men* production starts with the selection of fresh-harvested leaf sets consisting of one bud and either two or four leaves, depending on the quality requirements and tenderness of the leaves. Uniformly sized leaf sets and consistently tender leaves are selected. Too much variation in the base tea can cause uneven oxidation and diminish aroma, flavor, and color.

Keemun Mao Feng

In general, the production of black tea is more mechanized and automated than processing techniques for other top-grade teas. Freshly picked leaves are placed in special troughs to start the withering process. Depending on ambient temperature, moisture content, and leaf tenderness, warm air is piped in to maintain the required withering temperature

祁門紅茶

One of the daily essentials for almost everyone in Hong Kong is the "milk tea," a strong brew of black tea with a good dose of condensed milk added. Special milk tea stores and restaurants develop their own formulas and are supported by loyal customers who visit daily. The best milk tea is generally made with Ceylon black tea; anything else is considered low quality. On rare occasions during my Hong Kong childhood, my father would buy me a cup of milk tea along with an order of buttered milk toast (a thick toast coated with butter and condensed milk) from the small food stand near our house. He made sure that I knew that the stand used Chinese qi men *black tea instead of "that stuff from India" (he meant Ceylon, but my dad wasn't known for his geography prowess). Most Hong Kong residents are not as lucky as I was, though.*

I knew Anhui Province was one of the must-go tea destinations, with great teas like huang shan mao feng, qi men, liu an gua pian*—all among the ten most famous teas of China. How could I not be there? I finally visited the Qi Men tea* *factory to see the actual ins and outs of* qi men *tea making first hand.*

Like most people, I had thought, incorrectly, that the best grade of qi men *would be the famous* hao ya *(“furry tip”). Years ago,* hao ya *was so hard to get that only importers with great connections were able to acquire a chest or two; most people never got the opportunity. China has since lowered the standards dramatically, and* hao ya *teas in grades A to C are now widely available. What I discovered during my first visit to Qi Men was that there was an even higher grade of* qi men *called* li cha *(“gift tea”). The Chinese government selects this extra-special tea to be given to foreign dignitaries and diplomats. I have since pursued this great tea and have offered it to my customers.* Qi men *black tea is sometimes compared to fine wine (often called the “Burgundy of black tea”). It’s lighter in color than Indian black tea but no less in flavor; gentle and full of unique aromatics. Although less intense,* qi men *blacks are every bit as impressive as any other world-famous black tea.*

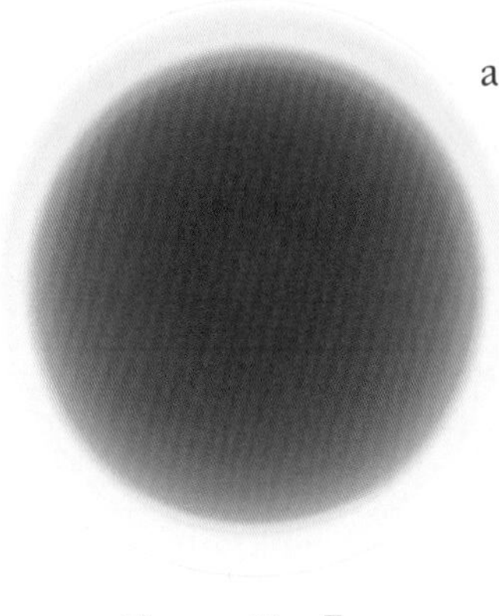

Keemun Mao Feng

and humidity until the leaves' moisture content is reduced to approximately 60 percent and the leaves start to darken and release a floral aroma. Next the leaves are processed with special machines that simultaneously roll and press them. Rolling is generally done in two stages: gentler at first to break down the cellulose structure, then the leaves cool and are rolled again with more pressure to release juice that coats each leaf's exterior. This process creates *bao guang* ("treasured luster") and allows the quick release of flavor and aromatics when the tea is infused. For the final oxidation 60–70 kilograms of leaves are placed in a fermenting trough where a temperature of 26°–28°C is maintained until the leaves oxidize to a reddish brown and a distinctive fragrance recalling ripe apples is released.

Finally, the tea is dried in hot-air roasting machines, first at approximately 105°C to lower the moisture level to 20–25 percent, then the leaves cool to avoid over-firing or charring the edges. Finally the tea is dried completely with a gentle firing in hot-air roasting machines at about 90°C, a process that takes the moisture to 5–6 percent. The leaves are graded by size and shape, broken leaves and stems are removed, and the finished tea is ready for packing and shipping.

Puerh

ALSO KNOWN AS

Bing Cha, Tuo Cha

Ancient records indicate that people of southwestern China have been producing, trading, and using tea in various forms for millennia, from boiling large leaves with spices to enjoy much like a soup, to steaming and molding the leaves into *tuan cha* ("compressed tea"), and later, to brewing it in loose-leaf form. It is reputed that during the Three Kingdom Era (220–265 AD), Kong Ming, the legendary strategist of the Shu Kingdom, discovered and cultivated tea in the Nannuo Shan area of Yunnan to help his soldiers fight exhaustion. Even today the minority tribal people in that region celebrate the legendary Kong Ming as a "Tea Ancestor." When Zhu Yuan Zhang, the first emperor of the Ming dynasty, decreed that no more *tuan cha* be made,

Chinese tea began to change from pressed to loose-leaf style. However, Yunnan's remote location allowed tea producers there to continue the tradition of compressed tea in various forms. For many reasons, it's no exaggeration to say unequivocally that *puerh* is unique in the tea world.

REGION

Puerh takes its name from the market town in the region where these teas are processed and sold. During the Qing dynasty, the ruling Manchu royalty prized *puerh*'s digestion-aiding properties and during the reign of Emperor Yong Zheng (1722–1735), *puerh* was officially made a tribute tea. A special official was appointed to Yunnan to supervise production and delivery of the best *puerh* to the court, and large amounts of tea were offered as tribute, a form of tax.

ON THE FARM

All *puerh* tea begins as *sheng cha* (green, or raw tea). In earlier times, Yunnan was a mountainous region and transportation of goods was very difficult. A "tea-horse road" was established to transport tea out of Yunnan. *Sheng cha* was carried on horseback, and the total time from harvest to consumers could be a year or more. *Puerh*'s high moisture content naturally promoted fermentation inside the burlap bags in which it was transported. By the end of the journey, *sheng cha* had naturally evolved into *shou cha* ("dark finished" tea). The result is a dark tea with a full bodied, deep red liquor and multiple layers of rich and complex flavor. *Puerh* is most popular in southern China and southeast Asian countries where the hot, humid climate often continues to re-ferment and change *puerh* stored there.

Sheng cha is produced by harvesting Yunnan's *da ye* ("big leaf") cultivar. The spring harvest starts in early March; this is the time to gather small leaf buds such as the ones used in Imperial Puerh, Jin Hao Puerh (golden tip *puerh*), and Yin Hao Spring Tip (small silver tips). Spring harvest typically ends around May 10; summer harvest starts right afterwards. Summer is considered lower quality, a time when any new leaf growth is picked rather indiscriminately. The final harvest is the autumn picking that lasts around 20 days, ending mid-to-late September.

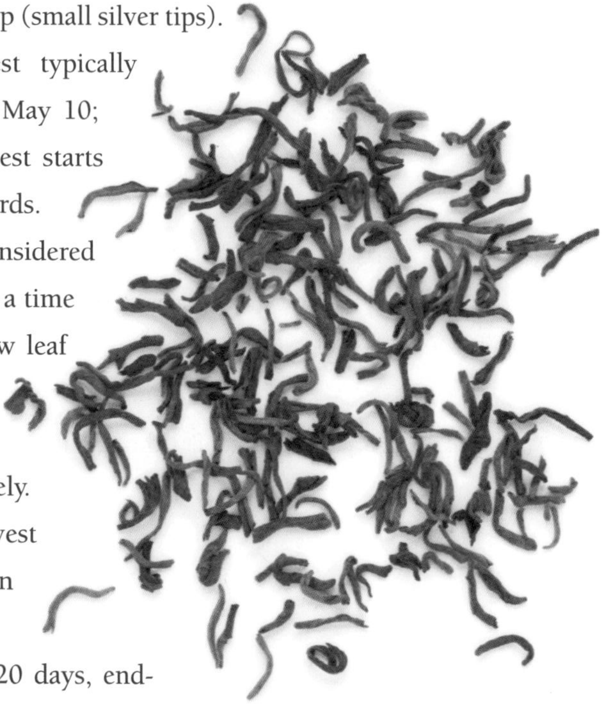

Imperial Puerh

普洱茶

I came in contact with this great tea early in my childhood, growing up in Hong Kong where the popularity of puerh *(which we Cantonese call* boh-lay*) is unequaled. Rich and poor alike there drink this tea regularly. When I was little, drinking aged* puerh *was a matter of course. Good aged* puerh *was abundant and affordable, so whether you were in a restaurant or at home,* puerh *was served. I actually began my journey as a tea professional by visiting Yunnan to negotiate an exclusive distributorship with the Yunnan Tea Import & Export Corporation. I still have* puerh *cakes that I collected from that trip.*

Unlike any other tea, puerh *is designed to be aged for years after harvest, and is regarded almost as a living being with personality. It displays one set of characteristics when young and continues to mature and change as time passes. As with a person, the environment in which it "grows up" affects the way it matures. This unique characteristic inspires passion and attachment to* puerh *unmatched by any other tea in the world.*

For every harvest the procedure is similar. The leaves are allowed to wither slightly, then go through the *sha qing* pan-firing process that cooks them through and stops oxidation. The leaves are then rolled into shape, and finally, put under direct sunlight to dry. Sometimes they're dried by placing them on bamboo mats suspended over a charcoal fire. *Sheng cha* tends to be harsh, bitter, and strong, and may also be very smoky due to this optional firing step. In time, however, these seemingly negative characteristics prove to be the tea's strength, providing more structure that allows it to age and mature.

1980s Shou Bing Cha

Sheng cha is also made into compressed forms, the most noted being the disc-shaped *bing cha* ("cake tea"), also called Chitsu Pingcha (Seven Son Cake Tea). *Bing cha* is produced by blending three different grades of tea: the attractive, tippy leaf goes on top, larger and initially harsh-tasting leaves form the core, and well formed smaller but less tippy leaves appear on the underside of the cake. To make the cake the leaves are placed in a cloth bag and steamed to make them pliable. The bag is then placed in a mold and pressed into the classic disc. Traditionally—and still occasionally today—cakes are pressed by placing a steamed bag of tea between two large stones. After pressing the pressed disc of tea is placed on a rack to cool, then moved to direct sunlight

1980s Shou Bing Cha

to dry. Some modern tea factories have a steam-heated drying room where compressed discs are placed on racks. The room's 35°–40°C temperature dries the cakes gently without adding smokiness.

Other compressed forms include *tuo cha* ("bowl tea"), a mushroom-shaped knob of compressed tea that comes in a wide variety of sizes. The production method is similar to *bing cha*. *Zhuan cha* ("brick tea") is a rectangular-formed cake pressed with larger leaves to produce a stronger-flavor blend that is popular with people from Tibet. Many other compressed teas are also produced, such as those stuffed into bamboo tubes and called Fragrant Bamboo Tea, as the tea absorbs the scent of the bamboo. Sometimes the stuffed bamboo is roasted over a fire until it splits open; the leaves are then taken out to be brewed.

The other type of *puerh* is *shou cha,* also produced in both loose leaf and compressed forms. Modern tea factories produce *shou cha* from *sheng cha.* Finished *sheng cha* is piled in a heap, then water is added and the pile is covered with a tarp. The moisture induces fermentation, which generates heat. The tarp is removed from time to time to release heat and moisture as needed. A long temperature probe is inserted into the pile to monitor it so the tea does not over-ferment. Periodically, the pile is turned and inspected. Under-fermented leaves display a mixture of green and reddish-black coloring, while over-fermented leaves are hard and black. Ideally fermented leaves have a brownish black color and yield a deep reddish infusion. When all the leaves have fermented evenly, the pile is spread out to allow moisture to escape. As the leaves dry, fermentation ceases.

STORING AND AGING

With green tea, temperature changes, moisture, and the passage of time are things to avoid. Most green teas are meant to be drunk as fresh as possible. While oolong and some black tea can be aged to an extent, they cannot withstand the unique aging techniques often applied to *puerh.* Thanks to *puerh*'s large leaf and high moisture content, temperature changes can actually be beneficial. At higher temperatures the leaf expands and releases moisture; *puerh* people think of this moisture as the life blood of the tea. With lower temperatures, the leaf contracts and reabsorbs moisture. This cycle allows *puerh* to coat itself repeatedly in its own juices, an action that continues to fuel bacterial and enzymatic activity within the leaf and ultimately transforms its color, aroma, and flavor. *Puerh* does best in semi-dry environments that experience significant temperature swings. Moderate dryness helps prevent excessive fermentation that can turn the leaf black and flavorless. Clean air is also needed, but too much air movement can disturb the aging tea's delicate balance.

Such an aging environment is sometimes called dry storage and results in slow maturation. However, especially with *sheng cha*, this method helps retain many of the most appealing qualities of a young *puerh* (notes of fruit, sometimes light floral notes, and strong multiple layers of flavors) along with the mature, full-bodied smoothness and pleasant sweetness of an aged tea. An almond-like nuttiness or a plum-like flavor can develop.

The time required to age *puerh* to maturity varies widely, depending on aging conditions and especially the tea itself. Smaller tips age a bit faster, while larger leaf *puerh* can remain almost unchanged for years. In the right environment, fine *puerh* can continue to improve for decades. Most tea experts now agree that storing *puerh* in an environment with excessive moisture is not desirable. This method is called "wet" storage and is meant to make a young *puerh* age faster; it can, however, produce undesirable flavors of mold, mildew, muddiness (if stored in a cave, for instance), and dirt.

PREPARATION

Many people think of *puerh* as a strong and robust tea; as a result, they always brew it with boiling water. However, each *puerh* is different and requires attention to its unique character. A tippy *sheng cha* can exhibit lots of fruit and a nice, sweet tannic quality. Brewing it with boiling water only brings out bitter astringencies that can overpower the delightful fruit and sweetness. It responds better if brewed much as you would brew a fine green tea, with water that's not too hot and only a moderate steeping time. More mature leaves require warmer—but still not boiling—water.

Shou cha responds to a different approach, because its fermentation process has typically removed some of the astringency you want to minimize in *sheng cha*. Hotter water brings out the full range of earthy, woodsy flavors and yields a light, sweet finish. A secret to enjoying *shou cha* is to brew it in hot water but allow the infusion to cool before you drink it, to bring out the full range of complex flavors but also optimize mouth-feel.

Well aged *puerh* is forgiving, complex, and silky smooth. Like an elder, it'll forgive you almost no matter what you do. Since the intensity has been smoothed out by aging, dark *puerh* can be prepared with more leaves and near boiling water. Green *sheng cha* is brewed more carefully, depending on how "green"; aged *sheng cha* that retains more of its youthful quality, such as light floral hints and fruitiness, should be brewed with lower temperature water. More full bodied and dark-color *sheng cha* requires higher temperatures to bring out the full range of complexity.

Imperial Puerh

周亮工 閩茶歌

雨前雖好但嫌新
火氣難除莫接唇
藏得深紅三倍價
家家賣弄隔年陳

楊錦銳書

Min Cha Ge (Min Cha Ballad)

by Zhou Liang Gong

Before the rain is desireable, but it's immature

The strong fiery flavor is hard on the lips

Worth three times more if stored till colored deep amber

Every family flaunts their years-old tea

Calligraphy by Yang Jing Rui

Zhou Liang Gong was an official in both the Ming and Qing dynasties.

Preparation Guide

The tea you drink is a collaboration between the artisans who made it and you. The leaves are just the beginning; it's their proper infusion in water that creates the beverage you will enjoy. Here are some basic principles for preparing tea. More details on each tea are in the respective chapters.

Water

Ninety-nine percent of tea is water, so it's important to select your water as carefully as you select tea. The best water for tea is an oxygenated spring water with a natural mineral content that's neither too hard nor too soft. Since mineral content varies greatly, you may want to do your own taste test of water available in your area to determine which seem most compatible with the tea you drink.

Properly filtered tap water can also be good. Distilled water is not recommended because it can produce a flat-tasting infusion. The best approach is to taste the available water before preparing the tea; if it doesn't taste good, find another option.

Teaware

GAIWAN

Because of its elegance, functionality, and ease of use the covered tea cup called the *gaiwan* has long been recognized as the universal tool of tea preparation. Made of porcelain, glazed stoneware, glass, or occasionally an exotic material such as jade, the *gaiwan* can serve to brew tea, serve it, or drink it. Its many virtues include a wide mouth that makes it easy to control temperature and view the evolving infusion, as well as an adaptability that works with every category of tea. There's also a real tactile pleasure in its superb ergonomics. It's the perfect vessel to begin your exploration of the captivating world of tea.

YIXING TEAPOT

The term *gong fu* tea refers to the skilled and knowing process for preparing tea, in which the teamaker brings spiritual as well as practical tea knowledge and experience to bear on enhancing the tea's strengths while downplaying its weaknesses. In a *gong fu* brewing session the teamaker responds intuitively to the water, tea, teapot, and environment, relying on a natural sense of harmony to brew the tea well. Traditionally *gong fu* preparation involves an unglazed teapot made from one of the special clays mined in the area of Yixing in China's southeastern Jiangsu Province. Well seasoned *yixing* teapots emphasize the importance of

continued practice as well as improve the flavor and character of oolong and aged *puerh*. Many connoisseurs reserve a separate *yixing* teapot for each variety of tea so that the pot becomes seasoned just to that type of tea.

OTHER TEAPOTS AND MUGS

If it's your preference, any number of teapots can be used to brew tea. Avoid metal if possible. For convenience, you can even brew tea directly in a cup or mug. The important thing is to adapt your preparation technique to get the most from every pot or cup of tea that you brew.

Temperature and Infusion Time

There is no "proper" water temperature and steeping time; these are variables that you control and adapt every time you make tea. Each infusion is an experiment and you can learn as much from failure as you gain from success. Other important variables include the amount of tea, character of the water, time of year, even the day's weather. The important lesson is that when you brew tea, you're the one writing the destiny for that cup of tea. Nevertheless, some beginners feel more secure with numerical guidelines, so to oblige, here are some general temperature ranges for the teas discussed in this book. However, I encourage you to ignore them and strike out to discover tea on your own terms!

Lukewarm: 50°C (122°F)
Warm: 60°C (140°F)
Very Warm: 70°C (158°F)
Medium Hot: 70°–80°C (158°–176°F)
Hot: 80°–90°C (176°–194°F)
Very Hot: 85°–95°C (185°–203°F)

General Tea Preparation

RINSE

Rinse all implements with hot water. This warms the teaware so the water temperature won't fall dramatically when you start to brew tea. It also protects fragile ceramics from sudden temperature changes that can cause cracks. Finally, rinsing the teaware cleans it. You should never need to clean your *yixing* teapots with anything except hot water or tea itself. After the rinse, discard the rinse water.

QUANTITY

Place the tea leaves nearby so that your tea brewing session can proceed without interruption as soon as the rinse is concluded. Tea is brewed by weight, not volume. For most brewing situations you'll want 3–5 grams of leaves. Leaf quantity suggestions that follow are based on 5 grams of weight (weight of leaf types varies greatly by volume, so adjust to taste).

AROMA

Before infusion, the leaves may be moistened with brewing-temperature water to bring out the aroma. Smelling the damp tea is not only pleasurable, it helps you decide how to brew and what brewing technique to use. For delicate white or green tea, moisten with only a few drops of water. For more robust teas such as oolong or *puerh*, completely infuse the leaves with water and immediately pour it off, a quick "rinse" that can also cleanse the tea of dust or broken particles that may have accumulated during processing.

INFUSION

Fill the *gaiwan* or teapot about 90 percent full, leaving a bit of space between the water and the rim to minimize spills. Except in the case of very delicate green tea, cover immediately. If you're brewing in an *yixing* teapot, pour a bit more hot water over the teapot to help equalize temperatures (this will also help your pot develop a nice patina). When your tea is ready, either pour it directly into serving cups or decant into a serving pitcher.

High quality, full-leaf teas can generally be re-steeped at least 2 to 3 times. For subsequent infusions try increasing the steeping time slightly and also use somewhat hotter water.

Recommendations for Specific Teas

WHITE TEA

For the mild but flavorful nature of *da ye* white tea, I recommend an infusion in hot to very hot water (3 heaping teaspoons for silver needle; 4 heaping teaspoons for white peony). Steep to taste, perhaps 2 minutes.

GREEN TEA

You may wish to begin brewing an unfamiliar fine green tea with water that's lukewarm to very warm. Start with 3 level teaspoons of leaves. Steep uncovered so you can watch the infusion develop for a minute or two. While a delicate green tea can be ruined in a stroke if it's stewed in water that's too hot, an equal danger is that you fail to appreciate the complex flavors and aroma due to an abundance of caution. At some point you should experiment with pushing the tea to the edge of bitterness to better learn its limits.

OOLONG TEA

For *dong ding*-style oolongs from Taiwan try 2 level teaspoons; for other Taiwan oolongs, try about 2 heaping teaspoons in medium hot to hot water and an infusion time around 1–3 minutes, depending on the amount of leaves used. For more oxidized and high-fired oolongs, including Wu Yi *yan cha* and darker *tie guan yin,* use hot to very hot water, again steeping 3 minutes or so (depending on intensity desired). Vary steeping time according to the quantity of leaf used.

PUERH TEA

Puerh is quite variable so it's hard to generalize. Younger, less fermented *puerh* can easily become bitter, so try about 2 teaspoons in medium hot water with a 1–3 minute steep time. Aged *puerh* probably requires hot to very hot water and an infusion time around 3 minutes. Refer to the *puerh* chapter, page 56.

BLACK TEA

Try very hot water with about 2 teaspoons of leaves and a 3 minute infusion. You may want to experiment with lower temperatures and longer steeping times.

Glossary

A Li Shan: An oolong tea-growing area in central Taiwan, known for its "high-mountain," or *dong ding,* style oolongs.

Anhui: A province in southeastern China, known for a wide variety of green teas as well as the black tea *qi men* (keemun).

Anxi: A county in China's Fujian Province, famed for its *tie guan yin.*

bai hao: "White fur." This term signifies a young tea leaf picked when it's still covered with abundant fur.

bai mu dan: "White peony." A true *bai mu dan* is a rare and exotic type of white tea from Fujian Province that meets the difficult standard of "three whites": the leaf set must possess one leaf bud covered in white down plus two leaves whose undersides are covered with white down and tops are dark green.

ban yan: "Half *yan cha,*" the designation for Wu Yi oolongs produced near but not in the best Wu Yi growing areas.

bao guang: "Treasured luster," referring to a glossy sheen on finished tea leaves that results when juice that has been squeezed from the leaves during processing coats them and dries; suggests a leaf that is full of flavor and nutrients.

bao zhong: A style of Taiwanese oolong grown in the northern part of the country, in the areas of Ping Lin and Wen Shan. Generally, the least oxidized type of Taiwan oolong. It is sometimes known in English as "pouchong."

Bao Shan: One of the prefectures in Yunnan Province where black tea is grown.

bi luo chun: One of China's most renowned green teas, from the Dong Ting Shan area, near Tai Hu, in Jiangsu Province.

bing cha: Cake tea, a form of *puerh* tea pressed into rigid, cake-like discs to facilitate transportation, storage, and aging. Also spelled beeng cha.

black tea: A fully oxidized type of tea known in Chinese as *hong cha* ("red tea") due to the reddish-brown color of the infused leaf and liquor. The dry leaf appears black, which is why it's called "black tea" in English.

blue oolong: A term sometimes applied by Western tea merchants to certain Taiwan oolong teas.

cai cha: Tea growing locally in the wild.

cake tea: See *bing cha*.

Camellia sinensis: The species of plant from whose leaves all true tea is made. Chinese teas are varieties of *C. sinensis* var. *sinensis*, while some black teas grown outside China are *C. sinensis* var. *assamica*.

chao qing: "Pan-fired green," a type of processing used for certain green teas.

Chong An: One of the areas where lapsang souchong is produced, in northwestern Fujian Province.

congou: A tea seller's term meaning leaf-grade tea.

da hong pao: "Big red robe," one of the most famous varieties of Wu Yi *yan cha*.

da ye: "Big leaf," a type of *C. sinensis* that produces larger leaves, from which oolong and *puerh* teas are made. Contrasts with *xiao ye* ("small leaf").

De Hong: One of the prefectures in Yunnan Province where Yunnan black tea is grown.

dian: An alternative Chinese name for Yunnan.

dian hong: "Yunnan Red," the black tea produced in Yunnan Province.

Dong Ding: A region that produces a popular style of Taiwan oolong.

Dong Ting Shan: The most noted growing region for *bi luo chun*. Dong Ting Shan is near Tai Hu (Lake Tai) in Jiangsu Province.

Dragon Well: See *long jing*.

Fan Zhong Yan: A Song dynasty poet who lived 989–1052. One of his famous poems discusses Wu Yi tea.

Feng Qing: A noted black tea producing area of Yunnan Province.

ferment: In biochemistry, fermentation refers to the process of energy production in a cell under anaerobic conditions. Among teas, only *puerh* and *liu an* experience true fermentation, during the aging process when microorganisms are active. However, the term fermentation is used informally in the tea trade as a synonym for oxidation, the processing stage when enzymes break down chlorophyll (causing the leaves to soften and darken) and transform tannins.

flag spear: See *qi qiang*.

Fo Hai: Historically, a *puerh*-producing area of Yunnan Province. Fo Hai is now known as Meng Hai.

Formosa Oolong: A highly oxidized style of Taiwan oolong noted for its honey-like floral notes.

fragrant bamboo tea: A type of compressed tea produced in Yunnan Province. The tea is stuffed into bamboo tubes, where it absorbs the bamboo aroma. Sometimes the tubes are roasted.

Fu Ding: An area of Fujian Province known for the production of fine white tea.

Fujian: A coastal province in southeastern China where the finest oolong, white, and jasmine teas are produced.

Fuzhou: The capital city of Fujian and the original home of jasmine tea production.

gaiwan: Traditional Chinese teaware that can be used to brew, serve, and drink tea. Fitting comfortably in the palm of the hand, a *gaiwan* consists of a saucer, bowl, and lid. The name means "covered bowl."

gong fu cha: Literally, "the work of making tea." The skilled and knowing process for preparing tea according to traditional Chinese practices, in which the teamaker brings spiritual as well as practical tea knowledge and experience to bear on enhancing the tea's strengths while downplaying its weaknesses.

gong mei: "Tribute eyebrows," a young, tender-leafed white tea with a smaller leaf and greener color than *shou mei*.

green snail spring: The English translation of *bi luo chun*.

green tea: One of many varieties of tea that are processed without allowing oxidation, so that the leaf remains green.

gu yu: A term applied to a certain harvest period before the spring rain and rice planting season begins around April 20.

Guangdong: A province in southern China whose primary tea production is oolong, black tea, and *puerh*.

Guangxi: A province in southern China situated between Guangdong and Yunnan. Because it offers lower costs, Guangxi is rapidly becoming the hub of jasmine tea production in China. The province also produces green and black teas.

Hangzhou: A major city in eastern China, the home of *long jing*.

hong cha: Literally, "red tea." The Chinese name for black tea.

hong qing: "Roasted green," a green tea production method in which the tea is roasted dry.

huang shan mao feng: A famous green tea from Anhui Province.

iron goddess of mercy: One of the many English translations sometimes seen for *tie guan yin*.

jasmine pearl: A type of jasmine tea in which the tea leaves are tightly rolled into small balls, or "pearls."

jasmine tea: Tea scented with fresh jasmine blossoms. Traditionally, jasmine tea is made with green tea.

Jia Qing: Qing dynasty emperor who lived 1760–1820. He succeeded his father, Qian Long.

Jiangsu: Province in eastern China, home of Tai Hu (Lake Tai), a famous green tea region.

jin hao: "Gold fur," designating a downy, early-picked leaf bud used to make Yunnan's *jin hao puerh* or top quality black tea.

Kang Xi: Qing dynasty emperor who lived 1654–1722 and was the grandfather of Qian Long. During his reign *bi luo chun* was designated a tribute tea.

keemun: Antiquated English spelling of *qi men*.

Kong Ming: A renowned Chinese strategist who lived 181–234. Among his many claims to fame, he discovered and cultivated tea in the Nannuo Shan area of Yunnan to help his soldiers fight exhaustion, helping to give rise to the *puerh* industry.

lapsang souchong: A variety of black tea from Fujian's Wu Yi Shan area.

Li Shan: A tea-growing area in central Taiwan, known for its "high-mountain" *dong ding* style oolong.

lian rui: "Lotus heart," a designation for the highest grade of *long jing*, picked very early in the spring and consisting of tiny single leaf buds sorted to a highly uniform size.

Lin Yin Temple: A famous Buddhist temple near Hangzhou. Some of the best Xi Hu *long jing* is grown near Lin Yin Temple.

Lin Cang: One of the prefectures in Yunnan where black tea is grown.

liu an gua pian: One of the most famous green teas from Anhui Province.

long jing: "Dragon well," one of China's best known green teas. The best *long jing* is produced near the city of Hangzhou.

lotus heart: See *lian rui*.

Mei Jia Wu: One of the top Xi Hu *long jing* production areas.

min: An alternative Chinese name for Fujian.

min hong: "Fujian Red," black tea produced in Fujian Province.

Ming dynasty: The Chinese imperial dynasty lasting from 1368–1644. The last dynasty when the country was governed by Han Chinese.

ming qian: The earliest harvest period for green tea, prior to the Qing Ming festival.

Nannuo Shan: One of the six famous *puerh* mountains, located in Xishuangbanna in southern Yunnan Province.

Nantou: A county in southcentral Taiwan, famed for its *dong ding* style oolong.

oolong: An oxidized *da ye* type of tea, noted for its potent floral character. Oolong is known in Chinese as *wu long* ("dark dragon") because some oolongs have a long, dark, twisted leaf shape.

Oriental Beauty: Another name for *bai hao* (Formosa) oolong.

oxidize: In tea, the process of enzymatically breaking down chlorophyll, which causes the leaves to soften and darken.

Ping Lin: A tea-growing region in Taiwan, known for its *bai hao* (Formosa) and *bao zhong* (pouchong) oolongs.

pouchong: Antiquated English name for *bao zhong*.

puerh: A *da ye* variety of tea from Yunnan. The name may be rendered with a multitude of spellings in English, including pu'er, pu er, bo lei, bonay, etc.

qi men: A black tea produced in Qi Men County in Anhui Province, generally known in English as *keemun*.

qi qiang: "Flag spear," a grade of *long jing* whose leaf-set comprises an unopened bud and a single leaf.

qi zi bing cha: "Seven son cake tea," a bundle of seven cakes of *puerh* tea, each weighing 357 grams.

Qian Long: Qing dynasty emperor who lived 1711–1799. He traveled extensively in tea-producing regions in southeastern China and his patronage significantly raised the reputation of several famous teas, including *long jing* and *bi luo chun*.

Qing dynasty: The last Chinese imperial dynasty, which lasted from 1644–1911.

Qing Ming: A festival in early April when Chinese remember their ancestors.

que she: "Bird tongue," or "sparrow tongue." A grade of *long jing* with a bud and two leaves that are slightly curled like a small bird's tongue.

seven son cake tea: See *qi zi bing cha*.

sha qing: A tea production process in which heat is applied to arrest further oxidation of the tea leaves.

shai qing: A production method where the final drying of the tea is accomplished by sunlight rather than with an artificial source of heat.

Shan Lin Xi: A tea-growing area in central Taiwan, known for its "high mountain" *dong ding* style oolong.

sheng cha: Unfermented *puerh* tea.

Sheung Wan: A Hong Kong district with many teashops.

Shi Feng: "Lion Peak," one of the most famous *long jing* production regions.

shou cha: *Sheng cha* that has been fermented, either through natural aging or by an accelerated process.

shou mei: "Longevity eyebrows," a larger-leafed white tea with a darker color than *gong mei*.

Si Mao: An important *puerh* production region in Yunnan.

silver needle: See *yin zhen*.

Song Bai Keng: Song Bai Village, an oolong production region in southcentral Taiwan.

Song dynasty: A Chinese imperial dynasty that lasted from 960–1279.

sparrow tongue: See *que she*. Sometimes called "bird tongue."

Tai Hu: Lake Tai, the largest freshwater lake in China, in Jiangsu Province.

tai ping hou gui: A famous green tea from Anhui Province.

Tang dynasty: Chinese imperial dynasty that lasted from 618–907, a period when China greatly expanded international trade. Tea was an important commodity in the country's flourishing economy during this era.

ti hua: A final scenting of jasmine tea that completes the lengthy process of scenting the tea leaves with jasmine flowers.

tie guan yin: A variety of oolong tea mainly produced in Fujian's Anxi County.

tribute tea: In dynastic China, a tea selected and produced for the imperial court.

tuan cha: Puerh tea that has been compressed into various forms.

tuo cha: A bowl-shaped compressed *puerh* tea.

Wen Shan: An important *puerh* production region in Yunnan, and an oolong-growing region in northern Taiwan.

West Lake region: See Xi Hu region.

white tea: A variety of lightly processed Chinese tea distinguished by two elements: the particular varietal—the da ye ("big leaf") variety, grown in Fujian's Zheng He and Fu Ding regions—and a specific production method.

Wu Yi Shan: A region in northwestern Fujian famous for its Wu Yi *yan cha.*

Xi Hu region: The area around Xi Hu (West Lake), a large freshwater lake in Hangzhou, where the most prized *long jing* is grown.

Xian Feng: Qing dynasty emperor who lived 1831–1861 and was the husband of Empress Dowager Cixi. During his reign large-scale, systematic production of jasmine tea began in Fuzhou.

xiao ye: "Small leaf," a type of *C. sinensis* that produces smaller leaves, from which most green tea is made. Contrasts with *da ye* ("large leaf").

xiao zhong: A *xiao ye* variety of black tea that's used to make lapsang souchong.

Xishuangbanna: A major *puerh* tea production area in southern Yunnan.

ya cha: Tea made from an unopened tea leaf bud. Contrasts with *ye cha*, made with the open leaf.

yan cha: A type of oolong that grows in the Wu Yi Shan region of Fujian.

yan yun: A term often used to describe the flavor profile of Wu Yi *yan cha.*

ye cha: Tea made from an opened tea leaf. Contrasts with *ya cha*, made with the unopened leaf bud.

Yixing: A city in Jiangsu Province famous for a specific type of clay used to make teapots.

***yin hao* spring tip**: Small, spring-harvested leaf tips covered in silvery white down and used to make top-quality loose-leaf Yunnan tea.

yin zhen: "Silver needle," a lightly processed Fujian white tea that is a *da ye* cultivar.

Yong Zheng: Qing dynasty emperor who lived 1678–1735, the father of Qian Long. During his reign *puerh* was officially named an imperial tribute tea.

yu cha: Lower-quality tea harvested after the spring rains begin in late April.

yu qian: See *gu yu*. Tea harvested before the spring rainy season begins in late April.

Yunnan: A province in southwestern China famous for its *puerh* and black tea.

Zhejiang: A major green tea producing province in eastern China, famed for its *long jing* tea.

Zheng He: A white tea producing region in Fujian.

zhou cha: Tea grown adjacent to Wu Yi Shan region.

zhu cha: "Pearl tea," known in the West as "gunpowder" tea.

Zhu Yuan Zhang: First and founding member of the Ming dynasty, who lived 1328–1398. During his reign *tuan cha*, or compressed tea, was outlawed, leading to the popularity of loose-leaf styles of tea.

zhuan cha: *Puerh* or black tea, from either Hunan or Yunnan, that has been tightly pressed into a brick shape.